THAN... CHILDREN'S BOOK

YOUR CHILD'S FIRST 30 WORDS

ILLUSTRATED BY:
FEDERICO BONIFACINI

ROAN WHITE

TEACH YOUR CHILDREN ALL THE NEW WORDS THEY NEED TO LEARN EARLY WITH THIS BOOK.

INCLUDING 30 OF THE MOST USEFUL, FUN, HAPPY WORDS, THIS COLORFUL, GORGEOUSLY ILLUSTRATED BOOK WILL BREATHE HAPPINESS AND PASSION FOR LANGUAGE INTO YOUR CHILD'S LIFE.

FROM MOM TO APPLE TO DOG TO RAIN TO PUDDLE, THIS BOOK BRINGS ALL THESE WORDS INTO YOUR KIDS LIFE THROUGH GORGEOUS ILLUSTRATIONS.

ALL VOCABULARY IS IN THAI.

แม่

พ่อ

พายแอปเปิ้ล

ช็อคโกแลต

โยเกิร์ต

แพนเค้ก

กอด

นก

น้ำ

ดาว

หมา

แมว

หนังสือ

ตุ๊กตา

กล้วย

สตรอเบอร์รี่

กระดานลื่น

ไก่

บ่อ

ตู้เย็น

คอมพิวเตอร์

ฝน

สายรุ้ง

จูบ

รถยนต์

บ้าน

เครื่องบิน

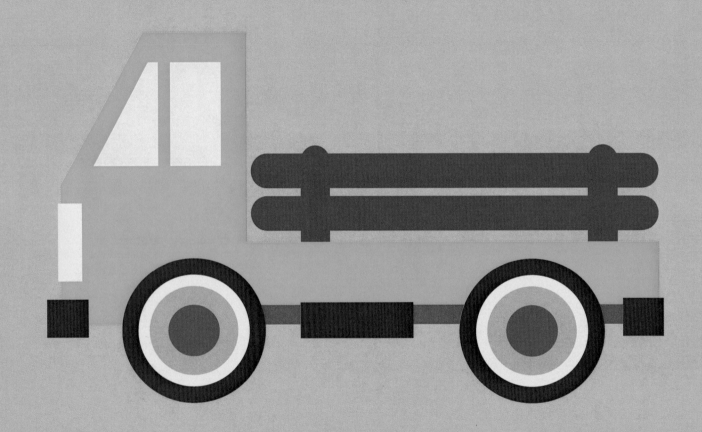

รถบรรทุก

สีเทียน

ทราย